James IV: King of Scots

A Tudor Times Insight

By Tudor Times

Published by Tudor Times Ltd

Tudor Times Insights

Tudor Times Insights are books collating articles from our website www.tudortimes.co.uk which is a repository for a wide variety of information about the Tudor and Stewart period 1485 – 1625. There you can find material on People, Places, Daily Life, Military & Warfare, Politics & Economics and Religion. The site has a Book Review section, with author interviews and a book club. It also features comprehensive family trees, and a 'What's On' event list with information about forthcoming activities relevant to the Tudors and Stewarts.

Titles in the Series

Contents

James IV: King of Scots

Introduction

James IV was the very ideal of a Renaissance Prince. Patron of learning, but skilled on the jousting ground, chivalrous lover of many ladies, yet a maker of pilgrimages, mighty in war and a dispenser of rapid justice.

He brought Scotland from a land of almost constant internecine warfare to a united country, able to raise an army equipped with the most advanced technology of the age, yet it was all lost, thrown away in a muddy field in Northern England by a man who was a great warrior, but an impulsive and foolhardy general.

James was one of Scotland's most successful kings. He united his country, enforced the rule of law, and showed that Scotland could take its place with pride on the European stage. The tragedy of Flodden and the chaos that the country was plunged into after his death have overshadowed his achievements. A charismatic, courageous and intelligent man, he deserves to be better remembered.

Part 2 contains James IV's Life Story and additional articles about him, looking at different aspects of his life. He was a man with a wide range of interests, taking part in intellectual and practical pastimes as well as the traditional jousting and military pursuits. He was also well-known for his colourful private life.

Family Tree

James IV
King of Scots

Widow on Bosworth child

James II
King of Scots
Born: 16 Oct 1430
Died: 3 Aug 1460

Mary of Guelders
Queen of Scots
Born: 1434
Marr: 3 Jul 1449
Died: 1 Dec 1463

James III
King of Scots
Born: 10 Jul 1451
Died: 11 Jun 1488

Christian I
King of Denmark
Born: Feb 1426
Died: 21 May 1481

Dorothea of Brandenburg
Queen of Denmark
Born: 1430
Died: 25 Nov 1495

Margaret of Denmark
Queen of Scots
Born: 23 Jun 1456
Marr: Jul 1469
Died: 1486

James IV
King of Scots
Born: 17 Mar 1473
Died: 9 Sep 1513

Margaret of England
Queen of Scots
Born: 28 Nov 1489
Marr: 8 Aug 1503
Died: 1541

Marion BOYD

Margaret DRUMMOND
Died: 1501

Lady Janet KENNEDY
Born: 1480 (app)
Died: 1540 (app)

Lady Isabel STEWART

James STEWART
Duke of Ross
Born: Mar 1476
Died: Jan 1504

John STEWART
Earl of Mar
Died: 11 Mar 1503

James V
King of Scots
Born: 10 Apr 1512
Died: 14 Dec 1542

Madeleine of France
Queen of Scots
Born: 10 Aug 1520
Marr: 1 Jan 1537
Died: 7 Jul 1537

II

Marie of Guise
Queen of Scots
Born: 22 Nov 1515
Marr: 18 May 1538
Died: 11 Jun 1560

Margaret ERSKINE
Died: 5 May 1572

Euphemia ELPHINSTONE

Elizabeth or Katherine CARMICHAEL

Elizabeth BEATON

Elizabeth SHAW

Alexander STEWART
Archbishop of St Andrews
Born: 1493 (app)
Died: 9 Sep 1513

Katherine STEWART
Countess of Morton
Born: 1494 (app)
Died: 1554

James DOUGLAS
3rd Earl of Morton
Born: 1490 (app)
Marr: 1543 (app)
Died: 1548

Margaret or Jane STEWART
Lady Gordon
Born: 1497 (app)

John GORDON
Lord Gordon
Born: 1500
Died: 1517

Alexander STEWART
Marr: 26 1517
Died: 13 Oct 1537

Sir John DRUMMOND
of Inverpeffray
Born: 1490 (app)

James STEWART
Earl of Moray
Born: 1500 (app)
Died: 1544

Lady Elizabeth CAMPBELL
Countess of Moray
Died: 1547

Lady Janet STEWART
Lady Fleming
Born: 1502 (app)
Died: 20 Feb 1562

Matthew FLEMING
3rd Lord Fleming
Born: 1489 (app)
Marr: 16 19 Feb 1524
Died: 10 Sep 1547

Henri II
King of France
Born: 31 Mar 1519
Died: 10 Jul 1559

TUDOR TIMES

James IV's Life Story

Chapter 1: Childhood

On 17th March 1473, Margaret of Denmark, Queen of Scots gave birth, probably at Stirling Castle, to the first of her three children. She had been married for four years to James III, but the couple were not happy. James III was a difficult man – a king from the age of eight, he had survived a long, factious minority, but, on attaining control of his kingdom had proceeded to alienate pretty much everyone in it. Even his brother, Alexander Stewart, Duke of Albany conspired with the English to depose him.

The young couple's first child was a son, named James for his father and grandfather. In fact, so popular was the name James with the king that the second son was given it, too, the third being named John. As the heir to the throne, this first James was given the title of Duke of Rothesay.

It appears that Margaret of Denmark was not entirely enamoured of the duties of married life, and would only sleep with the King in order to become pregnant. This reluctance, perhaps borne out of the fact that the wedding had taken place when he was seventeen and she just twelve, together with the fact that the Queen was more popular and capable than her husband (she was described as '*having more aptitude than he for ruling the Kingdom*') resulted in a less than warm relationship, although Margaret had brought a great deal to her new country. Unable to pay her dowry in cash immediately, her father, Christian I of Denmark, had pledged the Shetland and Orkney Islands. He never found the money, so the islands were ceded to Scotland.

Regardless of the state of their personal relationship, Queen Margaret stood loyally by James III when his brother, Alexander, Duke of Albany, who had escaped to France after being besieged by the King in Dunbar Castle, made an arrangement with Edward IV of England. England was to provide him with support in a bid for the Scottish throne and the price Albany was prepared to pay was the surrender of Berwick and other disputed border lands and an agreement to do homage to the English King.

In 1482, James III marched out to face Albany, who was backed by 20,000 English troops led by Richard, Duke of Gloucester (later Richard III). En route to Lauder in Berwickshire, which he had appointed as the meeting place for the feudal levies, the King was abducted in the '*Lauder Lynching*' by his own half-uncle, the Earl of Buchan and the Earl of Angus. Various of James III's supporters, who were looked down upon by the nobility for their lowly birth, were summarily hanged from the Lauder Bridge, and James III was taken back to imprisonment in Edinburgh Castle, under the wardenship of Lord Darnley, a known supporter of Queen Margaret.

This left Queen Margaret to negotiate with Albany. She was at Stirling with the nine-year old James, Duke of Rothesay, for whose education and upbringing she was responsible, as was traditional for Scottish queens. It can be inferred from the holding of James III in Edinburgh Castle, of which she was custodian, that Queen Margaret, if not actively involved in the abduction, was aware of the intention to rein him in. She was not, however, prepared to support his deposition. Queen Margaret and Prince James met Albany and negotiated around his desire to at least be nominated as Lieutenant General of the kingdom – effectively Regent. It appears that Hume and his colleagues were soon even less enamoured of the thought of Albany as king than James. Albany was just as rapacious as the king, and willing to submit Scotland to English overlordship, which James III, although he had pursued a pro-English policy, was not. That being so, Albany, to save face, besieged Edinburgh Castle, which quickly surrendered, allowing James to be set free.

James III therefore kept his Crown.

Soon, however, James and the lords were at loggerheads again. James had made a bitter enemy of Lord Hume - one of the most powerful Border lords, who commanded a significant portion of the eastern border with England. He and Hume had been in dispute about Church revenues and James decided to settle the matter by accusing Hume of treason, giving the latter the impression that his whole family was at risk of the King's vengeance. Hume's allies, including the Hepburns, began to fear for their own positions.

King James became suspicious of the motives of his son, despite the fact that Prince James had only been nine years old at the time of the abduction.

Prince James appears to have had a very close relationship with his mother who wished to inculcate in him the highest standards of princely behaviour. Allegedly, she taught him to wait upon her at the table, and bring her water to wash her hands, even though she had plenty of servants. This was to teach him the right way to command – mindful of his position, but not too proud. Nothing is known of his general education, other than that it must have been thorough and well-delivered, given James' later intellectual interests.

In 1486, Queen Margaret died, aged just 30, allegedly exhorting her thirteen year old son to the highest standards of kingship:

'When you succeed to your father's throne, above all else, love the people as yourself, with justice, mercy, generosity and affection...preserve the kingdom in peace and tranquillity...See that justice is not violated by greed...'

The Queen was buried at Cambuskenneth Abbey and Prince James remained at Stirling Castle, continuing his education.

Chapter 2: Rebellion and Coronation

Over the next two years, there was talk of a new marriage for James III, with Elizabeth Woodville – widow of Edward IV, and mother-in-law of Henry VII, the new English king. At the same time, the second Prince James, Duke of Ross, was mooted as a spouse for Katherine of York, daughter of Edward IV. The elder Prince James, previously considered for Katherine's older sister, Cicely, during the reign of her father, was not mentioned in these negotiations.

It may be that this promotion of his younger brother worried Prince James, or perhaps there was another cause, but on 2nd February 1488, Prince James left Stirling in secrecy to join a band of rebels, the chief leaders of which were Archibald Douglas, 5th Earl of Angus (known as Bell-the-Cat, although it is not a contemporary nickname), the Earl of Argyll and Lord Hume. James was probably aided and abetted by the Constable of the Castle, who was Hume's brother-in-law. King James, uncertain of his heir's whereabouts, realised that trouble was brewing and began to raise money for an army. Edinburgh and the south of Scotland were largely in the control of the nobles most dissatisfied with King James, so, on 24th March 1488, he marched north, to more loyal areas, to raise troops. He set up his base at Aberdeen and sent out requests for help to both England and France - it generally being politic for kings to help each other against disobedient subjects - but no help was forthcoming.

James III faced a growing group of rebels which encompassed the Humes, the Hepburns, the Earls of Angus and Argyll, the latter of whom had previously been a supporter of James, and even the Bishop of Glasgow. With the recruitment of Prince James to their ranks, they now presented a formidable opposition. The rebels also appealed to England for support, claiming, without any evidence so far as is now known, that James III, amongst other crimes and misdemeanours, had poisoned his wife.

King James still had a number of senior supporters, including his half-uncle, the Earl of Buchan, who although he had been involved in the *Lauder Lynching*, had returned to the King's side, and the chief prelate of the realm, the Archbishop of St Andrew's. The Archbishop, in particular, wanted to bring about a peaceful solution if at all possible.

Mindful that rebellion against the King was considered a sin, and should only be considered as a last resort, the rebels put forward a proposal for a negotiated settlement. Called the Articles of Aberdeen, the thirteen clauses, proposed some changes in behaviour on James III's part, including better maintenance and training of Prince James – he should be given mentors of *'wisdom and discretion...for the good governance of his person in his tender age.'*

The Articles were signed in May 1488, yet by early June the rebels were accusing the King of flouting them, although as they are rather vague, it is difficult to understand exactly what the King was expected to achieve in three short weeks. James began to march south, in part to reunite himself with his treasure – he was considered something of a miser, and, whilst debasing the coinage with cheap metals, stored gold in great chests for himself. Regardless of his personal affection for his gold, he would need it to pay any mercenaries sent by France or England.

James III headed for Blackness Castle on the Firth of Forth, in expectation of foreign troops who never arrived. The rebels appeared on his doorstep, and, leaving Buchan in charge, James slipped out the back door, crossed the Firth to the Port of Leith and re-entered Edinburgh Castle by mid-May. Now in possession of his chests of money and able to pay his troops, James emerged from the Castle and marched towards Stirling where Prince James and the rebels lay.

There were also rebels at Linlithgow, so James crossed again to the north side of the Firth of Forth to approach Stirling from the north-east. In a brisk skirmish, the King captured the town of Stirling and its Castle, but Prince James evaded his clutches. Fortunately for the Prince, the main part of the rebel army was approaching, and he joined up with it. The two forces now joined in battle – Prince James apparently issuing orders that his father was not to be harmed.

The forces met on 11th June. There is no contemporary account of the battle.

It is believed that King James had more men, and the sword of Robert the Bruce girded at his side, but neither of these factors could give him the victory. The loyalty of his men was questionable and what exactly occurred, either before, during or immediately after the battle is unclear. Neither side used artillery - it was a traditional man-to-man encounter, on ground that was surrounded by marsh. It seems to have been over very quickly, with the young Prince James being pronounced King James IV within hours.

What had happened to James III? There is no certainty as to whether he died on the battlefield or off it. One story is that the James III left the fray, either voluntarily, or because his horse ran amok. He then tumbled off the animal crossing the Bannockburn (rather a symbolic note to the tale.) On being carried to the nearby Beaton's Mill, he asked for priest.

One of the rebels, in disguise, entered the room and stabbed him to death.

On leaving the battlefield, James headed for Scone, where he was crowned on 24th June 1488. There was nothing hole-and-corner about the coronation, but it was conducted by the Bishops of Glasgow and Dunkeld, rather than the senior churchman, the Archbishop of St Andrews who had been a strong supporter of James III. Once James IV was crowned, the next step was to have his father buried. Two weeks after the battle, James III was interred at Cambuskenneth Abbey, not far from Stirling at the side of his wife, Margaret of Denmark.

The official enquiry into the King's death, held by James IV's first Parliament in October (almost the only indication that the battle actually took place) merely commented that James III 'happinit to be slayn' and that

> 'oure soverane lord that now is and the trew lordis and barouns that wes withe him in the samyne feild war innocent, quhyt and fre of the saidis slauchteris feilde and all persute of the occasioune and cause of the samyne'.

A reward for information on the identity of his killers, of 90 marks' worth of land, lies unclaimed to this day.

Whatever James IV's immediate feelings, he felt continuing guilt for his father's death, and, as penance, wore an iron belt around his waist for the rest of his life, adding a link each year – though whether that was to increase the penance, or the result of good living, who can tell? An entry in the accounts for six quarters of worsted to pad the belt suggests it was not as uncomfortable as all that.

James was still only fifteen, and thus, to some degree, controlled by the men who had rebelled against his father. The influence of the chief rebels, the Earl of Bothwell (who had custody of the minor king and his brothers) and Lord Hume was initially strong, and they gathered lands and offices as quickly as they could.

This was distasteful to the other nobles, such as the Earl of Lennox in south-west Scotland, and the Earl of Huntly in the north-east. Before long, Lennox and Huntly were in open rebellion. The plan was to abduct James, who was at Stirling.

James, always in the forefront of any action, rode out to meet the rebels and defeated them at the Battle of Gartloaning which took place just west of Stirling. Nevertheless, there was still concern about the stranglehold that Bothwell and Hume had over the Government. A new Parliament was called in early 1490, and the representation on the King's Privy Council was extended to a wider group.

Still disgruntled, however, was the Earl of Angus. He was cheered by two events – his appointment as Chancellor at the end of 1492, and his wife's niece, Marion Boyd, becoming the first of James' many mistresses.

In these early days, James began the journeyings around his kingdom that would come to characterise his reign. This was partly to make him seem as different as possible from his father, who had been disapproved of, in part, for his inclination to stay in Stirling or Edinburgh, surrounded by his particular favourites, rather than showing himself to his people and building relationships with his nobles.

However James IV was, by nature, an extraordinarily active man, and seldom stayed more than a week or two in any location, often moving on after a day or two.

He also soon showed an interest in naval affairs. The difficult terrain of Scotland necessitated frequent sea-travel and James became fascinated by ships and their potential as military weapons.

Another of James' trademarks was the frequency and thoroughness with which he carried out his role as giver of Justice. South of the Border, kings had stopped presiding over the courts some centuries previously, but this was still a key component of Scottish kingship. James was well-thought of for the thoroughness with which he would listen to the cases, and the generally wise decisions he made.

Chapter 3: Extending Scottish Influence

The Western portion of the landmass of Scotland and the islands off its coast had never been fully under the control of the Kings of Scots. Instead, they were the last remnants of the old Gaelic-Scandinavian kingdoms, ruled by their own Clan chiefs, and claimed variously by Norway, Scotland and Orkney. The Lordship was essentially a sea-kingdom, and its rulers depended on sea-travel in the galleys that were descendants of the Viking long ships.

By the early 1480s, the chief clan, Clan Donald, had weakened its position. It had accepted a Parliamentary forfeiture of some of its lands and a Royal Charter as the basis of holding the remaining territory. In addition, the clan chief, John Donald II, Lord of the Isles, had clashed with his illegitimate son, Angus Og. In 1488 and 1491, Angus Og and his cousin began raiding into lands outside the lordship, attracting the enmity of the Earls of Argyll, Angus and Huntly, and drawing Crown attention.

In 1493, Parliament declared the Lord of the Isles lands forfeit to the Crown, and James undertook an extensive tour in the region to emphasise royal authority. He arrived by sea in August 1493 at the royal stronghold of Dunstaffnage in Lorn. John Donald II submitted and was granted a pension. The following year, James visited again, and refurbished Tarbert, Loch Fyne and Dunvarty Castles. However, although John Donald II had accepted the Scottish King's overlordship, not everyone else in the Isles was equally happy.

The following years saw internecine feuding amongst Donald's family and clan, with no overall leader arising who could challenge James IV. From this time onward, the Lordship of the Isles never escaped its subjection to the Scottish Crown, despite later revolts in 1506-7.

One of the objections the Scottish nobles had had to James III was his inclination to a pro-English policy, rather the traditional alliance with France. James IV's councillors were not going to let him make the same mistake. In September 1491, the Auld Alliance with France was renewed. James' embassy, led by the Earl of Bothwell, was received at the French court in very honourable fashion by Charles VIII and his Chancellor, flanked by Bernard Stewart, Lord d'Aubigny, a distant cousin of James and Charles VIII's senior commander.

The delegation was treating with Charles about a possible marriage between James IV and Bianca Maria Sforza, sister of the Duke of Milan, but nothing came of it, and the Lady Bianca married the Emperor Maximilian as his second wife.

At the same time, James wanted to preserve the relationship with his mother's family, and throughout his reign he corresponded frequently with first his uncle, John of Denmark, and then his cousin, Christian II of Denmark. Relations with his grandmother, Mary of Guelders' family were also maintained.

Chapter 4: Hostility towards England

One of the most complex issues for Scottish kings to deal with was relationships with England. English kings frequently claimed overlordship of Scotland, and contenders for the Scottish throne were usually willing to grant it, in theory, at any rate, in return for English troops. Scottish kings had to resist this, often indulging in low level incursions across the Border that were designed to annoy, whilst not provoking their larger neighbour into outright war.

There was also the constant lawlessness in the Border territory. *"Reivers"* was the term used for the wild Border clans of both sides, living in the *"Debatable Land"*, ie in areas with no fixed border between the countries and minimal royal authority. *"Reiving"* is basically cattle-rustling but they did not confine themselves to cattle and murdered, raped and robbed each other, or any passer-by who fell into their hands, of any animals or goods quite cheerfully. This state of anarchy was often winked at, if not actively encouraged, by the nobles who were supposed to control it.

By and large, the Scots population was strongly opposed to cordial relations with England, but some of the nobles, in receipt of pensions and bribes from England, were willing to challenge this attitude. In particular, the Douglas Earls of Angus were often pro-English in their policy.

James IV began with the popular pro-French stance. His overarching ambition was for Scotland to be recognised as an independent state, definitely not subject to English suzerainty. To do this, he needed to build links with other countries, persuading them to see him as a powerful ruler. The major concern in 1490s Europe was the growing power of France, and its attempts to dominate the Italian peninsula, and, in exchange for detaching Scotland from its alliance with France, other European rulers were prepared to indulge James in his ambitions.

Ferdinand and Isabella, sovereigns of Spain, wrote to their ambassador in Scotland:

'The Scots have such a very good opinion of themselves as to pretend that they can induce the King of France to restore the counties of Roussillon and Cerdaña to Spain. Puebla can therefore say that they shall have an Infanta of Spain as soon as they effect the restoration of the said counties. They will not be able to do it, and will lose much time in unpleasant negotiations, which perhaps might end in a quarrel with France. At all events, pending the negotiations, they would not assist France against Spain.'

For James, as for all mediaeval and renaissance kings, warfare and increasing his military might was a part of the job, and he took to it with gusto. A seven year truce had been signed with England in 1493, reflecting the pro-English stance of Angus and Bishop Elphinstone, but, his confidence boosted by success in the Isles, James grabbed the chance presented by trouble south of the Border in the 1490s to raise his profile on the European stage.

Henry VII was plagued by a young man claiming to be Richard, Duke of York, son of Edward IV. The man, whose real name was probably Perkin Warbeck, had been received with all honour in France, Burgundy and other parts of the Empire. He had failed, however, in his first attempt to invade England, and was now looking for more support.

Scotland in the early days of James' reign had been cautious about getting involved, and was actively discouraged from doing so by the Spanish sovereigns who wanted to maintain peace between England and Scotland. Now, James decided to welcome Warbeck with open arms. The young man was treated as a prince and married to Lady Katherine Gordon, daughter of one of James' chief earls.

Over the following eighteen months, Warbeck received Scottish support, culminating in an invasion, led by James and Warbeck in late summer of 1496. Warbeck, appalled by the reality of war, left after a

day's campaigning, but James pressed on. His aim was the re-capture of
Berwick.

For a few weeks, James and his well-equipped troops made trouble
for England, destroying castles between the Rivers Tweed and Till and
giving Norham Castle a severe battering. In late September, the English
army, under Thomas Howard, Earl of Surrey, left Newcastle. James,
retired back over the Tweed, pleased with his summer's work, especially
as he had taken enough plunder to pay for the campaign.

Henry VII was by no means an aggressive king, but he would not
tolerate incursions into his territory. With an enormous sum in taxation
voted by Parliament, Henry set about raising an army to teach James a
lesson. James stayed close to the Border over-wintering at Melrose
Abbey and readying his artillery for war.

James owned the massive gun, *Mons Meg*, by far the largest artillery
piece in the British Isles. *Mons Meg* was capable of doing spectacular
damage with its eighteen-inch diameter 330lb cannon balls that could
travel well over a mile and a half. *Mons Meg* was brought up from
Edinburgh Castle and fitted with new wheels, ready to trundle into battle.
The host was summoned for June 1497. There were efforts from both
Spain and France to make peace between the countries, but, at this stage,
neither King was prepared to back down.

In May however, Henry hit a snag as the £120,000 in taxes voted by
Parliament came to be collected. Cornwall rebelled. The threat was so
serious that Henry quickly looked to make peace with Scotland, even
though the Cornish revolt was defeated by mid-June.

In July, Warbeck was provisioned by James with a ship to sail to
Ireland or the West of England, where he failed to make any headway
and was captured. James, meanwhile, with his army now arrayed, was
showing his strength. Henry had sent three ambassadors to treat with
his Scottish counterpart, including Bishop Richard Fox, one of his chief

Councillors. James, with his levies arriving for the previously agreed June meet, declined to treat. He besieged Norham Castle with Bishop Fox inside and did significant damage to the fabric.

Before the Castle could be forced to surrender, Henry's army, under the Earl of Surrey advanced, so James, deciding to quit while he was ahead, retired to Edinburgh. Surrey did not pause at the border, but marched on to besiege Ayton Castle, the property of Lord Hume.

The majority of James' army had now finished its service and dispersed. However, he marched out again with as many troops as he could find. Surrey, although with more men, was not well provisioned. The two armies drew up, some twelve miles apart and their leaders sent aggravating messages to each other, with no real intent of coming to a pitched fight. Rather provokingly, James challenged Surrey to single combat, the winner to take Berwick.

The Earl, who was in his late fifties, compared with James' twenty-four, wisely declined, saying that although he was honoured that a king would fight a mere earl, Berwick belonged to his master and he could not pledge it.

Both armies retired, but James had shown himself as a successful leader with the resources and skill to cause Henry VII annoyance and unpleasant expenditure. He was thus in a position to make peace on good terms. A seven year truce, the Truce of Ayton, was signed on 5th September, pending a more comprehensive treaty.

Chapter 5: Peace & Prosperity

As part of James' plans to bring Scotland to centre-stage in Europe, he had negotiated throughout the late 1480s and 1490s for a suitable Queen.

Bianca Sforza, sister of the Duke of Milan had been one possibility, and he even went so far as to ask for the hand of Marguerite of Austria, widowed daughter of the Emperor Maximilian. He tried for a Spanish princess, but was offered only an illegitimate daughter of Ferdinand, the pill of illegitimacy to be sweetened with a fat dowry.

The peace with England, however, led to a different choice – James was to marry Henry VII's eldest daughter, Margaret. Princess Margaret was a mere eight years old at the time of the Truce of Ayton, but the eventual agreement, known as the Treaty of Perpetual Peace and signed on 24th November 1502, agreed the union and assigned a very impressive dowry of £10,000 English for Margaret. In return, she received a jointure from James of land and rents of £2,000 Scots per annum, plus a further £1,000 Scots as a spending allowance.

With his mark made on the European stage, and the Treaty with England in place, James, in the opening years of the sixteenth century, was free to spend his time on other things.

He busied himself with architectural projects. James spent significant sums of money on turning the old hunting lodge at Falkland into a Palace fit for a renaissance monarch, adding the great hall at Stirling Castle and largely renovating Linlithgow.

He began the transformation of Holyrood Abbey into a Palace, surrounded by fruit orchards and pleasure gardens, the site for which was created by draining the adjacent loch in 1507. Architecture was not just an indulgence; it was a statement of power and wealth. Henry VII had recently constructed the new palace of Richmond, and James could not afford to fall too far behind in the magnificence stakes.

James also pursued his other interests, which were as varied as dentistry, embroidery and alchemy. Most exciting of all for the King, the Queen and his courtiers was the great tournament of 1507.

During this period, however, domestic tensions mounted as James, who was extravagant, began to outrun his income. His demands for taxation weighed heavy on his nobles, although there was no outright defiance. Part of the money he raised was devoted to the development of Scotland's naval power.

Chapter 6: Scottish Navy

The discoveries in the New World by Spain and Portugal in the latter quarter of the fifteenth century gave rise across Europe to an increased interest in ships and naval affairs. James was no exception to the rule, and he became fascinated by ships from the start of his reign, frequently visiting the dockyards at Leith, the port of Edinburgh.

Ships were also important for the protection of trade. James was descended from Mary of Guelders, and trade with the Low Countries had always been an important aspect of the Scottish economy. Unfortunately, Scottish merchant shipping often suffered from the depredations of English piracy.

In 1489, five English ships had sailed up the Firth of Forth and ravaged Leith and Fife. James and his councillors could not overlook this and issued Letters of Marque (effectively a commission to a private ship's captain to act on behalf of the Government) to Sir Andrew Wood, who confronted and trounced the English ships off Dunbar, with his two merchant vessels. Henry VII sent three men-of-war, but Wood saw those off, too.

This success encouraged James in his liking for ships, and all sea-towns were commanded to build ships of twenty tons, with "*vagrants*" to be pressed as crew. This sudden increase in ship-building required more timber than was available. Supplies were purchased from Norway and

France and in 1503 an Act of Parliament was passed commanding every laird to plant an acre of woodland. Additional timber was procured from France in 1506, on the understanding that the Scottish navy would be at King Louis XII's disposal.

The two most important vessels for this nascent navy were the *Michael*, and the *Margaret*. The *Michael* was the largest ship afloat in the first quarter of the sixteenth century. At a length of up to 240 feet (c. 70 metres) and breadth of 56 feet (c. 17 metres) she was an impressive sight. Her crew consisted of 300 gunners and she could carry upwards of 1,000 fighting men, as well as 27 bronze guns and 300 smaller pieces of artillery. At a cost of some £30,000 Scots, she cost James about a year's income.

As well as the aforementioned Sir Andrew Wood, James had another seaman (or pirate) on whom he could rely to create tension. Andrew Barton and his brothers had been granted Letters of Reprisal against Portuguese shipping, by James III. A Letter of Reprisal was a licence to take measures against any shipping carrying the flag of a country that had offended the recipient. Barton sailed up and down the English Channel, and on more than one occasion captured shipping of countries trading with Portugal.

In 1507, James gave Barton another Letter of Reprisal as well as Letters of Marque, but it was clear Barton was soon overstepping his authority. In 1508, Barton was captured by the Emperor's men, and only personal intervention by James in 1509 secured his release. Undaunted, Barton captured an English ship heading for Portugal. James, embarrassed, revoked the Letter of Marque, but Barton ignored him and proceeded to take an Antwerp vessel. James ordered him to pay compensation, but there is no record of him doing so.

Barton was then lent to James' uncle, John, King of Denmark, in his bid to control Sweden, in return for timber. He continued to be a liability, leaving King John's service without permission, taking the ship James had lent with him.

By 1511, almost everyone was fed up with Barton. The Englishmen, Sir Thomas Howard and Sir Edmund Howard, sons of James IV's old antagonist, the Earl of Surrey, took to the seas to capture a man who was now bordering on piracy. The Howards were successful, killing Barton and taking possession of the *Lion* and the *Jenny,* the former of which went into the English navy.

James demanded redress, in accordance with the Treaty of Perpetual Peace, but was put off. He continued to pursue the matter, although not with any great vigour, but the incident damaged the relationship between Scotland and England. Henry VIII loftily informed James that kings did not involve themselves in discussions about pirates.

Chapter 7: Road to Flodden

The Treaty of Perpetual Peace also aimed to deal with the constant low-level lawlessness of the Borders. There were supplementary treaties that dealt with the Border courts (long in place to deal with the day to day issues), and the redress that each king could expect if the behaviour of the Reivers became too outrageous.

Murders were to be dealt with by courts with juries manned from both sides. It was agreed that, provided the relevant king handed over any miscreant for proper punishment, incursion into the other realm would not be considered an act of aggression.

Throughout the remainder of Henry VII's reign, the terms worked reasonably well, and peace between the countries enabled even the Borders to know some level of proper government.

This changed with the accession of Queen Margaret's brother as Henry VIII. Henry VIII was a man most unlike his father – fed on tales of chivalry, he dreamed of military victory in France and English overlordship of Scotland. Although the Treaty of Perpetual Peace was renewed in 1509, it soon became evident that Henry was not interested in maintaining good relations with his sister's husband.

In both the Andrew Barton affair, mentioned above, and other border matters, he failed to give the redress required by the treaty. He also withheld the legacy left to Queen Margaret by either her father, or late brother, Arthur. Most worrying of all, he encouraged insulting statements in the English Parliament about James being his vassal.

In 1511 James asked Pope Julius II to release him from the Treaty of Perpetual Peace, claiming that England had broken its terms on several occasions. The Pope refused as Anglo-Scottish affairs did not occur in a vacuum and wider issues were at stake. The perpetual Italian Wars that ravaged Europe throughout the first half of the sixteenth century affected everyone as alliances came and went.

By 1511, the line-up was Pope Julius II, allied with Spain, the Empire and England against France, supported by Florence. Julius wanted to do everything he could to minimise France's allies. He made it clear that James risked excommunication if he broke the Treaty himself and attacked England. Julius may have hoped that James, as a particularly devout son of the Church, would be reluctant to defy him in the matter.

James IV had made concerted efforts to broker peace between France and the Papacy. He had many times declared his desire to go on Crusade and believed that war in Europe should be avoided in order for Christians to unite against the Infidel. Such an idea tends to make modern people smirk rather cynically, but there is no real reason to doubt the sincerity of the religious feeling of the time. In particular, the fall of Constantinople in 1453, and the incursions being made by the Ottoman Turks in Hungary, had caused concern in Christian Europe.

James was notably superstitious in his religious practice, even by the standards of the time and, as aforementioned, continued to feel guilt over the death of his father. Creating a peace settlement that would enable Christians to repel the Turks would surely have earned him heavenly forgiveness. Unfortunately, no-one else was interested in peace and when the French declared a Council of the Church at Pisa in 1512 which appeared to threaten the Papacy's spiritual leadership, the die was cast for European war.

James was in a cleft stick. He had a long term obligation to France, renewed in 1507, but he also had a treaty with England and risked excommunication if he broke it. In retrospect, it is simple to say that he should have kept quiet and not allowed himself to be drawn into the war, but that was not easy. Unfortunately, he could not please both Henry VIII and Louis XII of France. Both kings demanded support, specifically they both wanted to charter James' ship the *Michael*.

Henry was delighted to be offered the ostensibly legitimate excuse of protecting the Pope's spiritual leadership to lead an invasion into France. In June 1513, he set sail. Meanwhile, the French were pressing James to attack England. Louis tried a two-pronged approach. His Queen, Anne (herself the victim of French depredations in her own duchy of Brittany) sent James a turquoise ring from her own hand and pleaded with the chivalrous James to be her knight. Louis offered a rather more tangible incentive, sending 50,000 French Crowns to fund an invasion.

James was probably not sorry to take the opportunity, as he thought, of teaching a lesson to the twenty-two year old Henry, whom he doubtless felt to be a young whipper-snapper. It seems likely he thought he could repeat his successful raids of 1496-7 and return to Scotland unscathed. Despite the misgivings of some of his nobles and according to later stories, Queen Margaret begging him to desist, James invaded England in support of his obligations to France under the Auld Alliance.

For the third time James was heading over the border – this time with an army reckoned at some 42,000 men, the largest ever raised in Scotland. Norham Castle fell in six days, followed by Wark, Etal and Ford.

James' opponent on the final battlefield was not Henry himself, who was still campaigning in France, but the Earl of Surrey, whom he had faced back in the late 1490s. In a combination of skilled generalship by Surrey, who used his knowledge of James' brave and impetuous character well, and James' determination to press his early victory home, rather than quitting whilst ahead, the enormous Scots army, well equipped and with the odds strongly in its favour, was decimated. James and many of his leading nobles were slaughtered on the field.

It was sometime before James' body was identified amongst the thousands dead. In the end it was recognised by Lord Dacre, English Warden of the West March and taken to Berwick. From there, it travelled to Surrey, to Sheen Priory in a lead-lined coffin.

James had been excommunicated in the summer of 1513, as threatened by Pope Julius II, the sentence being carried out by Cardinal Bainbridge, Archbishop of York – hardly a neutral figure! This excommunication caused some difficulty in burying James, as, in theory, an excommunicate could not be buried in sacred ground.

Henry VIII, showing a modicum of Christian charity to his brother-in-law, wrote to the Pope, requesting permission to bury James IV:

'As it is to be presumed the King gave some signs of repentance in his extremities, the Pope allows him to be buried with funeral

honours, trusting the oversight thereof to Richard [Fox] bishop of London, or some prelate chosen by the King.'

It was planned that James would be buried as befitted a king, at St Paul's Cathedral, however, that never happened and his body was left in a store-room at Sheen. There it remained for over fifty years, until it was opened and the body desecrated in Elizabeth's time. The head was, apparently, rescued by the Queen's Glazier, who arranged for it to be buried at the Church of St Michael at Wood Street, central London - a site now graced by the Red Herring Pub.

Aspects of James IV's Life

Chapter 8: James IV's Personality & Appearance

The most obvious characteristic about James IV that shines through every mention of him in Ambassadors' correspondence, his own actions, and the records of his reign, is his boundless energy. James was constantly on the move, seldom staying in one place for more than a few days, racing around his country, by both horse and ship, popping up unexpectedly in far-flung corners of the realm and dispensing largesse liberally.

Although not an especially tall man, his physical prowess was remarkable – his favourite party trick being the ability to leap into the saddle of a running horse. This vigour was reflected in his enjoyment of the traditional pastimes of gambling, hunting, hawking and jousting.

James' energy was not just physical, it was mental as well. He was widely read, fluent in several languages (including Gaelic) and encouraged both poetry and music at his court, playing and listening to musical instruments, such as harps, clasarchs, shawms and lutes. He rewarded the foremost poet of the age, William Dunbar, extensively, paying him an annual pension of some £80 Scots.

Literacy and education generally seem to have interested James. In 1496 the first act for compulsory education in the British Isles was passed, when all landowners were required to educate their sons in grammar (Latin) and law. His own illegitimate son, Alexander Stewart, was tutored by the most famous Humanist of all, Erasmus. The new printing press, too, was patronised by the King and during his reign myriad books on a wide range of topics were published.

A pastime that James apparently enjoyed, that would be unusual in the twenty-first century for a man who seems so masculine in his tastes, was embroidery and fine needlework. Perhaps he was so energetic that it was impossible for him to sit without doing something with his hands.

James took a keen interest in medical matters. According to Pitscottie he was:

'weill learned in the art of medicine, and was ane singular gud chirurgiane [surgeon]; and there was none of that profession, if they had any dangerous cure in hand, but would have craved his advyse'

Not content with giving surgical advice he actually got personally involved in dentistry - paying people to allow him to extract their teeth!

As James' power and influence grew, he became determined to create a suitable setting for his majesty. The old hunting lodge of Falkland was transformed into a Renaissance Palace, complete with gardens and tennis courts, and liberal sprinklings of James' thistle badge, which was coming to be synonymous not only with him personally, but with Scotland. Linlithgow, too, received a modern makeover and Stirling a new Great Hall.

Technology fascinated James, particularly military advances. The army he took across the Border in 1513 was equipped with the very latest in weaponry and tactical developments. Naval matters, too, were extremely important to him. Henry VIII has often been referred to as the father of the British Navy, but, in reality, James IV was there before him with his two enormous ships, the *Great Michael* and the *Margaret*, and he frequently visited the dockyards at Leith.

James may have been a modern king in many respects, but he was extremely traditional in the practice of his religion. As well as his penance of the iron belt mentioned earlier, he went on numerous pilgrimages to the various holy sites and shrines in the realm. When his Queen, Margaret Tudor, was ill following the birth of their first child, he undertook a pilgrimage on foot, to the shrine of Saint Ninian, some 120 miles from Edinburgh, to pray for her recovery; giving alms at the outer kirk, the rood, the altar, the high altar, the altar of Our Lady and the relics. The walk was sufficiently hard for him to need his shoes re-soling, at a cost of 16d.

An important aspect of kingly behaviour that obviously came naturally to James was the giving of extravagant 'drinksilver', charity, and monetary presents for the little tributes that his people brought to him. The records show frequent payments such as the 14s given to a 'poor maiden', another 14s to a woman who brought him butter at Stirling and 9s to a child who brought apples.

The most delightfully profligate expenditure of all was the 4s paid for wine to bathe the hooves of the horse owned by the tournament champion, Sir Anthony D'Arcy.

In 1498, James was described by the Spanish Ambassador, Pedro de Ayala:

The King is 25 years and some months old. He is of noble stature, neither tall nor short, and as handsome in complexion and shape as a man can be. His address is very agreeable. He speaks the following foreign languages; Latin, very well; French, German, Flemish, Italian, and Spanish; ... He likes, very much, to receive Spanish letters. His own Scots language is as different from English as Aragonese from Castilian. The King speaks, besides, the language of the savages who live in some parts of Scotland and on the islands. It is as different from Scots as Biscayan is from Castilian. His knowledge of languages is wonderful. He is well read in the Bible and in some other devout books. He is a good historian. He has read many Latin and French histories, and profited by them, as he has a very good memory. He never cuts his hair or his beard. It becomes him very well. He fears God and observes all the precepts of the Church.'

He may not have cut his hair or his beard in 1498, but that soon changed when he married! His young wife objected to the hirsute look and so, the morning after his wedding he was ceremoniously shaved by Queen Margaret's chief lady-in-waiting, Agnes Tilney, Countess of Surrey, and her daughter. The ladies received sumptuous presents in return for their labours.

The very few images available of James show him clean-shaven, so either date from after his marriage or are stylised.

Whilst James' enthusiasm and eagerness to be first in everything was an attractive trait, it was one that, in the end cost him his life. By the late fifteenth century, it was becoming unusual for a king to stand in the forefront of battle, instead they acted as generals at the rear, but James insisted on showing leadership in the traditional way.

'He is courageous, even more so than a king should be. I [Ambassador Pedro de Ayala again] am a good witness of it. I have seen him often undertake most dangerous things in the last wars. On such occasions he does not take the least care of himself. He is not a good captain, because he begins to fight before he has given his orders. He said to me that his subjects serve him with their persons and goods, in just and unjust quarrels, exactly as he likes, and that therefore he does not think it right to begin any warlike undertaking without being himself the first in danger. His deeds are as good as his words.'

Had James taken a more circumspect position at Flodden, rather than throwing himself into the thick of the battle, he might have lived to fight another day. But he died as he had lived – extravagantly, bravely and whole-heartedly.

Chapter 9: James IV's Wife & Four Mistresses

James IV took delight in the physical pleasures of life – music, poetry, rich foods, gambling, tournaments and food. This enjoyment of the physical included a love of women. He was well-known for having a string of mistresses. These women were not, however, just passing fancies (although there were some of those) but were also political statements. A mistress could rise and fall with her family and a change in the King's companion could signal a change in his policy. It seems that unmarried Scottish ladies of good birth were prepared to enter into relationships with the king, or other nobles – which was rather different from England, where such affairs would be considered disgraceful.

James' first 'official' mistress was Marion Boyd. Marion was the niece-by-marriage of Archibald "Bell-the-Cat" Douglas, 5th Earl of Angus. Angus had been involved in the rebellion that overthrew James III, but, suspect for his pro-English stance, had been side-lined by Bothwell and Hume in their initial control of James IV's government. Angus, one of the richest and most powerful nobles in Scotland, found a way around his exclusion by keeping James company at the dice and card tables. It would have been easy for him to introduce Marion to the King. The affair lasted for about three years, from 1492 to 1495, during which period Marion bore two children, Alexander Stewart and Katherine Stewart.

James acknowledged the children and Alexander was given the education of a prince, although a prince destined for the Church, not the throne. Following the grant of the dispensation necessary to overcome his illegitimacy, he became a sub-deacon, and at the early age of eleven was nominated as Archbishop of St Andrews.

This was a most inappropriate appointment and was an example of the blatant abuse of the Church for political ends, but there was minimal protest and James found the revenues from the appointment came in useful for replenishing the royal coffers. Alexander's early education took place in Scotland, but when he was about fourteen, he travelled to France, the Low Countries and Italy. It was in Padua that he studied under Desiderius Erasmus, who wrote:

'..how quick, how attentive, how eager he was!...though he was a youth scarcely eighteen years old, he excelled as much in every kind of learning as in all those qualities that we admire in a man.'

Alexander perished at Flodden, with his father.

Marion Boyd's daughter, Katherine, was married to James Douglas, 3rd Earl of Morton, and bore several children.

In 1495 Marion fell from favour. She was found a husband, John Muir of Rowallan, and James found a new mistress.

Margaret Drummond, James' new love, was the daughter of John, Lord Drummond, and the sister-in-law of the Earl of Angus' son, George. Margaret took up residence in Stirling Castle and later at Linlithgow. It is unclear how long the relationship lasted and it was even suggested later that James and Margaret Drummond had been secretly married, although there is no contemporary evidence for this.

By 1501, Margaret was back at her father's house, where she died shortly after, together with two of her sisters. It seems the sisters were poisoned, whether accidentally or deliberately, is unknown. Cases of poisoning could, of course be natural, in a time with no refrigeration. Rumour at the time was divided between accusing the King's Councillors who wished to get Margaret Drummond out of the way to encourage James to marry Margaret Tudor, or accusing the husband of one of the sisters of wanting to get rid of her, and the deaths of the other siblings merely being fall out.

James IV's wife, Margaret Tudor, believed (or purported to believe – the man in question being her enemy) that the sisters were poisoned by Lord Fleming. Writing in 1523, she said

'For the Lord Fleming, for the evil will that he had to his wife, caused to poison three sister, and one of them his wife, and this is known of truth in all Scotland.'

Whatever the truth of the matter, King James paid for masses for Margaret Drummond's soul.

In 1496, a daughter had been born to Margaret Drummond, Margaret Stewart, whom James clearly doted on. The little girl had quarters at Edinburgh Castle with a nobly born governor and governess, a good sum for her board and attendance, and costly clothes. The only aspect of her education of which there is any evidence, is a payment for dancing lessons. In 1510 the thirteen year old Margaret was married to Lord Gordon, heir of the Earl of Huntly.

Widowed in 1517, with three children, she made two subsequent marriages, and had a further six children.

After Margaret Drummond's dispatch, whether by fair means or foul, James seems to have had a short relationship with Lady Isabel Stewart, daughter of the Earl of Buchan and thus a distant cousin. Lady Isabel had a daughter, Janet Stewart, who had a colourful career as governess to Mary, Queen of Scots, and mistress of Henri II of France.

The timing of this relationship with Isabel Stewart is difficult to understand – Janet Stewart's birth date is given as 1502, yet she definitely had the affair with Henri II in the late 1540s, giving birth in

1551 to Henri d'Angouleme. It is not impossible for a woman to have a child at the age of 49, but it is extremely unusual. This, together with the fact that her Christian name was Janet, rather than Isabel, might mean that she was, in fact, the child of James' final relationship of note, outside marriage.

This last liaison was with Janet Kennedy, daughter of Lord Kennedy. Janet Kennedy was married young, to Alexander Gordon, a distant relative. Janet and Alexander seem to have separated not long after the marriage and she began a connection with Bell-the-Cat Earl of Angus (yes – him again, he pops up everywhere!) The status of the relationship is unclear, as she is not referred to as his Countess, but he made grants of land to her, for her life, and for the benefit of any children they might have together. Some 30 years later, Janet referred to Bell-the-Cat as her husband when founding a charitable position, for the welfare of his soul. Since Angus was, at the time, married to Elizabeth Boyd, it is all rather confusing.

Whatever Janet's relationship with Angus, she certainly became James IV's mistress sometime in the late 1490s. The relationship lasted for several years, and she lived with him throughout the period of his marriage negotiations. On the arrival of his bride, Janet was granted Darnaway Castle, near Inverness, for her life, provided that she remained 'without husband or other man'. James continued to visit Janet at least until 1505, when she married again, although she was divorced by 1508. Janet bore two or three children to James: their son was James Stewart, 1st Earl of Moray, and they probably had two daughters, one of whom at least is presumed to have died young.

However much James loved his various mistresses, there was no question of his marrying any of them. A king's marriage was a valuable commodity, and James intended to make the very best use of a card he could only play once.

During the 1490s negotiations for various foreign princesses were undertaken. One possible bride was Bianca Sforza, sister of the Duke of Milan. Another contender was the daughter of Frederick of Aragon, King of Naples, but as she was a baby in the 1490s, this was not a practical suggestion.

More serious negotiations took place with Spain. James would have been delighted to marry a Spanish Princess, both for the prestige, and also to strengthen ties with England, where Katharine, the youngest Spanish Princess was promised. Ferdinand and Isabella were willing to offer Ferdinand's illegitimate daughter, with a good dowry, but were less keen for a marriage with one of their legitimate girls. Nevertheless, they strung James along for a while to keep him out of the arms of France.

'Doña Juana is a natural daughter born before marriage. If the King of Scots know this, and nevertheless likes to marry her, her marriage portion might be doubled...If the Scots wish to have one of the Infantas of Spain they must be put off with false hopes, because if a plain refusal were given them they might be induced to reconcile themselves with the King of France.'

Eventually, however, it was settled that James should marry Margaret, eldest daughter of King Henry VII of England. The marriage would be the living symbol of the new Treaty of Perpetual Peace – the first peace treaty between the countries since the late fourteenth century. The only slight fly in the ointment was Margaret's youth. When the treaty was agreed she was well under the minimum marriageable age of twelve.

Polydore Vergil, historian of Henry's reign, recorded that Henry's Council raised a concern that marrying his daughter into Scotland would

risk a later King of Scots becoming King of England. Apparently Henry
replied equably:

> 'What then? Should anything of the kind happen (and God avert the
> omen), I foresee that our realm would suffer no harm, since England
> would not be absorbed by Scotland, but rather Scotland by England,
> being the noblest head of the entire island, since there is always
> glory and honour in the less being joined to that which is far the
> greater, just as Normandy once came under the rule and power of
> our ancestors the English." And so the king's wisdom was praised
> and they unanimously approved the measure. Margaret was
> betrothed to King James.'

A dispensation for the marriage was granted by the Pope on 28th July
1500. This was required as James and Margaret were both descended
from John of Gaunt. The Treaty was signed on 24th January 1502 with
Margaret taking part in a proxy marriage at Richmond the next day,
where James was represented by the Earl of Bothwell.

It was agreed that the full marriage would not take place immediately
but would be delayed until the bride was at least 13, which would be 28th
November 1502. The reason for the delay was Margaret's youth. Her
grandmother, Margaret Beaufort, matriarch of the Tudor dynasty, had
been married at about the age of twelve and given birth to Henry VII at
about thirteen. She described this early child-birth as having 'spoyled'
her, rendering her incapable of further child-bearing. She was adamant
that her young grand-daughter should not suffer the same damage,
particularly as the girl was described as very slight and small, clearly
taking more after her father's family than her tall, robust, golden-haired
Yorkist mother. Henry explained the reason for the delay to Don Pedro
de Ayala, the Spanish Ambassador,

'The Queen and my mother are very much against the marriage. They say if the marriage were concluded we should be obliged to send the princess directly to Scotland, in which case they fear the King of Scotland would not wait, but would injure her and endanger her health'

Eventually, Princess Margaret left Richmond Palace with her father on 27th June 1503 to be married to the 30 year old King James IV.

On her progress to her new kingdom, Margaret lacked nothing in the way of material comfort and splendour. Her father had fitted her out with a huge wardrobe, jewellery and horses. More personally, in a rare survival of evidence of personal affection from the time, he gave her a Book of Hours, inscribed in his own handwriting in two places:

'Remember yr kynde and loving fader in yr prayers – Henry R'

and

'Pray for yr lowving fader that gave you this boke and I gyve you at alle tymes godd's blessyng and myne. Henry R'

Henry accompanied Margaret as far as Collyweston in Northamptonshire, then on 8th July she parted from her family to head north, accompanied by a great train of ladies and gentlemen, including her grandmother's husband, the Earl of Derby. The leader of her entourage was Thomas Howard, Earl of Surrey, but his was a short term role, just to take her to Scotland and see her safely married. Her permanent household was to be led by Sir Ralph Verney, her Chamberlain, and his wife Eleanor Pole.

Despite all of this splendour one can imagine the fear and trepidation in Margaret's heart as she processed grandly through all of the cities on the Great North Road, greeting dignitaries and being royally entertained. She had just lost her mother in childbirth, an ordeal that could not be too far away for her, and she was to be married to a man she had never seen, much older and more experienced than herself. She is likely to have known that James, unlike her faithful father, was a womaniser.

Margaret finally arrived at the border at Berwick on 30th July 1503. She was met by the Archbishop of Glasgow and a host of her new subjects, including a clutch of trumpeters to blow her a fanfare. At Dalkeith, two days before her official entrance to Edinburgh, in keeping with tales of chivalry, James 'accidentally' met Margaret whilst purporting to be on a hunting trip. Fortunately, he was wearing a smart crimson velvet jacket, rather than anything more workaday.

James greeted his bride warmly and spent the two days putting her at her ease, quickly discovering a shared interest in, and aptitude for, music. On departing from her, he could not resist the opportunity to impress her with his favourite party trick – the ability to take a running leap onto his horse

Feeling safe in his masterful horseman-ship, on the 7th August Margaret made her official entry into her new city riding pillion behind James, to the delight of the crowds. He had first tried his own horse with a pillion on which was mounted a servant, to check whether it was safe for Margaret. The horse objected, so the saddle and pillion were put on her gentler palfrey.

James and Margaret were married at Holyrood Abbey, Edinburgh, on 8th August 1503 and Margaret was crowned following the nuptial mass, James holding her around the waist for much of the ceremony.

As a wedding present for Margaret, a Book of Hours was created, perhaps commissioned by James himself. It was the work of several hands, probably made in Ghent, with the most famous contributor likely to have been Gerard Horenbout, court painter to Margaret of Austria, Regent of the Low Countries. There is a portrait of James, perhaps taken from a known likeness, but Margaret is a more stylised figure.

James treated his young wife both courteously and kindly, granting her Kilmarnock as her morning gift and buying her clothes and jewels. However he did not feel the need to break off his relationship with Lady Janet Kennedy. He may have continued the relationship partly because he seems to have been considerate enough to spare Margaret immediate consummation (although the accounts of their wedding state that they retired to bed together.) Her first pregnancy was not until 1506, resulting in the birth of a son, named James, on 21st January 1507 and christened on the 23rd of that month at Holyrood.

James was generous in his joy, giving £90 to the 'Lady Maistres' who had given him the news, £7 to Margaret's mid-wife and £14 to the baby's nurse. The rapid christening may suggest that the baby was not strong and after the birth both Margaret and baby James were dangerously ill. King James was genuinely fond of his wife and her dangerous illness

'grevit him sa sair that he wald not be comforted: nouther of man wald receive ony consolatione.'

This was the occasion on which he took the pilgrimage to St Ninian's shrine, mentioned above. Perhaps through divine intercession or perhaps on account of her own youth and strength, Queen Margaret recovered, but, after initial improvement, the baby died within a year. She went on to have four more pregnancies by James; two prior to the birth of James V on 15th April 1512 ended in still birth, with her final child by James being Alexander, Duke of Ross.

During his marriage, although James does not seem to have replaced Lady Janet Kennedy with an official mistress, there are quite a few payments to a woman named as Jane 'bare-arse' in his accounts – we can probably guess what services were being provided!

After the succession of Queen Margaret's brother as Henry VIII of England, relations between the two royal families deteriorated. Henry withheld money due to Margaret under her father's will, and generally behaved in a way calculated to annoy James. Margaret supported her husband throughout the dispute, but she must have suffered when it became apparent that the nation of her birth and the country of which she was queen were heading for war. There were stories later that Margaret begged James not to fight, and that she retired to the tower of Linlithgow Palace, to watch and wait for the husband who never returned from the battlefield of Flodden.

Chapter 10: James IV and Tournaments

Tournaments, in which men competed both individually and in teams, were the late mediaeval sporting equivalent of modern motor racing – so expensive that only the richest could take part, adrenaline fuelled, dangerous, and guaranteed to impress the ladies.

The sport had developed in the Middle Ages as a genuine preparation for battle, with severe injury and death amongst the protagonists not uncommon when the bouts were held '*a l'outrance*' – that is, to the uttermost. By the end of the fifteenth century the activities were more stylised, with concentration on skill as much as strength, and proceedings were usually stopped before the death blow.

The great tournaments held in the Courts of Europe during this period were occasions for pageantry and display, as well as sporting prowess. Frequently, skilled combatants from across Europe would take part. It was not unusual for kings to take part personally, if they were sufficiently talented. The Emperor Maximilian I was a noted combatant.

James IV was as keen on tournaments as any king of his time, and spent considerable sums on armour. He had his own armourer, Alan Cochrane, but he also sent his armour to France for repairs and brought specialist armourers from France to supplement his own craftsmen.

Tournament armour was phenomenally expensive – made to measure, it was often elaborately decorated – unlike the more workaday models worn in battle. No pictures exist of James' armour exists but there are several extant suits belonging to Henry VIII, showing the different fashions over the first half of the century. A suit of jousting armour could weigh as much as 100lb (about 45 kg).

In accordance with custom James would announce a tournament to be held and invite

'all and sindrie his lordis, earleis, and barrouns (quhilk was abill for justing or tornament to come to Edinburgh to him, and thair to exerceis themselffis for his plesour as they war best accustomit, sum to rin with speir, sum to fight with the battell axe and harnis, sum to feight with the tuo-handit suord, sum to shut the hand bow, corsebow, and collverine [an early type of hand-gun].'

Valuable prizes were given, reflecting the specific sport – thus the winner of the spear-throwing would receive a golden, ceremonial spear. Even more pleasing in an age when reputation for physical courage was important, the King's heralds would proclaim the winner as the best in the realm.

One of the jousting heroes of the age was a Frenchman, Sir Antoine D'Arcy, later Sieur de la Bastie, and known as the *'White Knight'* – possibly from the colour of his armour, or perhaps because he wore a white scarf in honour of Anne of Brittany, Queen of France. Sir Antoine appears to have been reading the recently printed Arthurian romances, as he wandered round Europe, in the fashion of a knight from Camelot, challenging all comers.

Sir Antoine arrived in Scotland in September 1506 for a stay of four months. James extended lavish hospitality to the knight, who was lodged with one James Aikmen, paid 21s per week from the King's coffers. Not only was Sir Antoine's accommodation paid for, various small expenses charged by Aikman to a total of 42s were covered.   There was also payment for food, for himself and his retinue, and a very large present of £112 before Christmas of 1506.   Even more extravagantly, James paid for wine to bathe the hooves of Sir Antoine's tournament horse.

The White Knight's challenge was taken up by Lord Hamilton.   The honours appear to have been even, although in rather sore-loser fashion, D'Arcy claimed to have been suffering from an '*indisposition of body*' on the day when Hamilton won a clear victory at Falkland Palace.

In the New Year of 1507, a further round of tournaments was held at Stirling, with the King, the Queen and the Court in attendance.   It would appear that Sir Antoine was again the victor as he received £280 in cash. In an early episode of "re-gifting", the King also presented him with ten silver goblets which had been given to James by the Bishop of Moray, and a gold salt-cellar that Queen Margaret had given to her husband.   These precious items were accompanied by a silver service from Flanders, costing £150 and a silver bowl and flask.   Sir Antoine, no doubt well pleased with his rewards, was overtaken on his way home by further gifts from the King, including seven French saddles.

The tournament of the Black Knight and Lady, one of the great set-piece pageants of James' reign, took place in the summer of 1507.   The tournament was announced by Marchmont Herald, to take place in the lists (the tournament ground) at Edinburgh Castle.   The event was to last five weeks and the idea was that the Black Knight and his supporters would prove his Lady to be the fairest in the land, at the point of a sword.

A large silk pavilion was set up, with a couple of smaller canvas ones. From the top fluttered various standards of taffeta.   In the grounds was set the Tree of Esperance (hope), planted in the garden of Patience and bearing the leaves of Pleasure, the flower of Nobleness and the fruit of Honour.   Over the five week duration of the event, each week the shield of a new challenger was hung on the tree. This again suggests familiarity with the Arthurian romances – illustrations in the 12th century manuscripts by Chretien de Troyes show just such an arrangement. The pavilions had fringes of silk and painting the shields and blazons required six books of fine gold leaf.

James himself was to be the defending Black Knight. Parts of his sumptuous costume were delivered from London in a couple of locked trunks. His outfit included a gold clasp for the gorget that encircled his throat and an arming jacket (presumably worn under the armour) of black satin. His squires were dressed in cloth-of-gold and black velvet with matching bonnets (caps) and hose. Payments for silver horns suggest that his armour might have looked something like the helmet presented by the Emperor Maximilian to Henry VIII in 1514.

The Black Lady (who was probably black in fact, as well as name) was dressed in a gown of damask with flowers of gold. The dress was decorated with yellow and green taffeta and the Lady sported leather gloves. She was carried in some sort of litter, imported from Flanders, which was draped with around 160 yards (160 metres) of Flemish taffeta in various colours. The Lady had four attendants – two squires, dressed in white damask, and two girls, clad in more yellow taffeta. The horses, too, were sumptuously decked out.

As well as the contests between the King's defending party and the challengers, there were pageants and shows involving painted canvas dragons, which had saddles and reins, suggesting they were to be ridden in some way, and men dressed in goat skins.

Although there are no details of exactly how the tournament played out, the King was, (not altogether surprisingly!), the winner and claimed the Lady's hand as his prize.

So successful was the event, that it was repeated the following year, on an even grander scale. By staging spectacles of this sort, James was showing, not just that he was sufficiently master of his country to spend time on leisure, but that Scotland's court and nobles were the equivalent in skill and sophistication of Burgundy or France.

Chapter 11: Following the Footsteps of James IV

James IV lived the life of a peripatetic mediaeval monarch. He hardly ever remained in one place for more than a few days, or weeks at most.

There was a pattern to James' year, which reflected the passing of the seasons, the timing of the sessions of Justice in Ayre, the important religious celebrations, and the location of his current mistress. A typical year in James' life would have had an itinerary something like that below which is based on his activities in the year 1505. The numbers in the brackets show the locations on the maps which follow.

The year opened with the King in Edinburgh Castle (Residences 2). He made a trip to the Chapel at Restalrig, (Abbeys 19) where he bought some honey. He left the capital in February, to travel to Stirling Castle (Residences 1), which was the most centrally located of his Palaces, and the probable location of his birth. It is certainly where he spent his youth, prior to defeating his father at the Battle of Sauchieburn (Military 34).

En route to Stirling, he stopped at Linlithgow, (Residences 3) which he had spent considerable time and effort on renovating, and which was the favourite palace of his wife, Margaret of England.

In March James returned to Edinburgh, then left for Lochmaben (Military 47) to see the building works at his new castle. He travelled on to Dumfries, where he relaxed by listening to a local singer, 'the crukit vicar'. He then moved on to Peebles, where he must have stayed in a

very grand inn as it cost him 42s. Whilst there, he bought a mule –
although for what purpose is unrecorded.

A quick return was made to Edinburgh Castle, followed by visits to
various shrines, including Whitekirk (Abbeys 33), near Dunbar Castle
(Residences 5) and the Ladykirk of Steill (Abbeys 24) which he had
founded following his successful Border campaign in 1495.

He was back in Edinburgh for Maundy Thursday (or Skyre Thursday
as it was known), where he performed the usual charitable activities. He
also gave 28s to a poor woman from the north, who was trapped in
Edinburgh, pending a decision in a legal case. The law was not much
swifter then, than now!

Off he went again, to Stirling, where he paid an extravagant tip for the
delivery of butter, and bought some gloves from a '*maiden*', most likely
the daughter of his usual glove-supplier. A flying visit was paid to
Falkland Palace (Residences 6) around the 7th May, but he soon returned
to Stirling, having visited the shrine at Tillicoultry (Military 45). From
Stirling he went to Dunblane, and returned to Edinburgh by 23rd May to
hear High Mass at Holyrood (Residences 7) on the feast of Corpus
Christi.

James then visited one of his favourite places – the Port of Leith
(Military 35), where he inspected his shipping, dining on board a boat on
27th May – his silver plate having been sent for him to eat off.

The next location was Dumbarton Castle (Residences 8), where he
was involved in preparations for a siege against a rebellious Walter
Stewart, taking refuge in Lord Hamilton's house. Other than a two day
trip to Glasgow and Paisley, the court remained at Dumbarton until 15th
June. The return to Stirling was via Ayr, Auchinleck and Craigbernard.

By the end of June, the King was back in Edinburgh, again giving alms
to the unfortunate, before returning to Dumbarton by mid-July. He

followed this up with a visit to Lord Sempill's new chapel (Residences 16), where he made a donation of 14s before returning to Ayr and then visiting the Abbey of Crosraguel (Abbeys 27) and the Abbey of Glenluce (Abbeys 31). James was interested in gardening and we find him giving 14s to the gardener at Mytoun, home of Sir Alexander MacCulloch.

On the last day of July, the King was at the shrine of St Ninian, Whithorn (Abbeys 22). This shrine was dear to James' heart. When his Queen was very ill, following the birth of their first child, this was the shrine he walked to, barefoot, to pray for her recovery.

The night of 2nd August was spent at the monastery of Dundrennan, in return for an offering of 20s. He went on from there to Dumfries and Lochmaben again.

Travelling around the country with the number of attendants usual for a king could create problems, especially if the Court hunted or hawked as they travelled. During this August, compensation had to be paid for damage done to growing corn. Given the difficulty of growing sufficient grain in Scotland, it is unlikely that a cash payment would have cheered the farmer much.

To enhance his hunting pleasure, the King received a present of a couple of dogs: payment had to be made for someone to lead the animals back to Edinburgh. Hunting also required the purchase of copious arrows. An eye-watering gift of £4 was given to Richard Grey, Earl of Kent (Queen Margaret's first cousin, once removed) who gave James a present of bows and arrows.

James was at Stirling by mid-August, where he received the news that the final instalment of the Queen's dowry had been delivered – no doubt welcome news, as the King's expenses continued to out-run his income.

A late August hunting trip then took place – it was probably men only as the party slept in tents. Food supplies included presents of butter and curds from two country women, pike and eels from the Prior of Inchmaholme and pears from the Laird of Buchanan. James was not a gluttonous man, so simple food would have sufficed him. A quick visit to Dumbarton was squeezed in before returning to Stirling where the Court was entertained by a Spanish riding display.

The King returned to Edinburgh where the High Kirk (Abbeys 20) was celebrating the feast day of its patron, St Giles on 1st September. He would have attended the High Mass and watched the celebratory procession through the streets, the effigy of the saint being carried high on men's shoulders.

Hunting again occupied his time from 3 – 5th of the month.

Later in September, James was travelling in the south east, visiting the border town of Ayton, where the Truce of Ayton had been signed in 1497, and inspecting the works at Ladykirk again, giving '*drinksilver*' to the various workmen. He also found time to visit Whitekirk (Abbeys 33), where he played cards.

The final weeks of September were divided between Edinburgh and Stirling, before James travelled to the great Abbey and Palace at Dunfermline (Residences 12), followed by Falkland, Perth (Residences 14), Methven (Residences 9) and Dundee. Whilst he rested at Dundee for a day or so, his hawks and dogs continued north, to meet him at Arbroath before moving on to Montrose and Brechin. He continued north to Strathbogie and then went for a day or so to Darnaway Castle (Residences 10), which he had given to his mistress, Lady Janet Kennedy.

James moved on to Inverness, before crossing into the Highlands to visit the shrine of St Duthus at Tain. His journey south included another brief stop at Darnaway, before a visit to Aberdeen. Progress had slowed somewhat, and the dogs and hawks were again sent on ahead.

James was back in Stirling on 31st October, before travelling to Edinburgh where almost all of November was passed, perhaps in contemplation of the wolf that had been sent to the King as a gift!

Christmas was passed at Holyrood, before the whole cycle began again.

Key to Map 1: Royal and Noble Residences

1.   Stirling Castle

2.   Edinburgh Castle

3.   Linlithgow

4.   Scone

5.   Dunbar Castle

6.   Falkland Palace

7.   Holyrood Palace

8.   Dumbarton

9.   Methven

10. Darnaway Castle

11. Jedburgh

12. Dunfermline

13. Dunbar Castle

14. Perth

15   Inchinnan Palace

16. Castle Semple

The main royal palaces were concentrated along the River Forth, between Stirling and Edinburgh, but James spent a good deal of time visiting the castles of his nobles, or other Royal Burghs, such as Perth and Ayr.

Map 1: Royal and Noble Residences

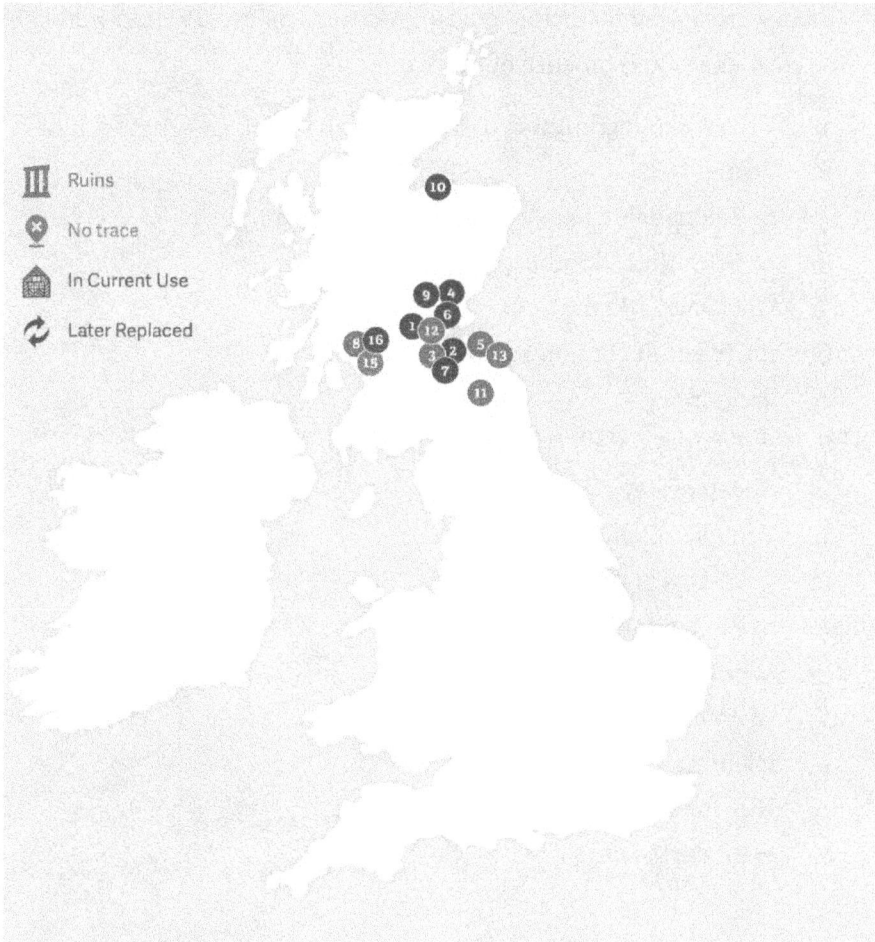

Key to Map 2: Abbeys, Priories and Places of Pilgrimage

James was an indefatigable pilgrim, visiting Abbeys, Priories and holy places the length and breadth of his realm.

1. Cambuskenneth Abbey
2. Scone
3. St Triduana's Chapel, Restalrig Edinburgh
4. St Giles Kirk, Edinburgh
5. Glasgow Cathedral
6. Shrine of St Ninian, Whithorn
7. Jedburgh
8. Ladykirk of Steill (Upsettlington)
9. Sheen Priory
10. Dunglas (Collegiate Church)
11. Crossraguel Abbey
12. St Michael, Wood Street
13. Whitehaven Priory
14. St John's Church Tower Ayr
15 Glenluce Abbey
16. Kilwinning
17. Whitekirk, Dunbar

Map 2: Abbeys, Priories and Places of Pilgrimage

Key to Map 3: Military

James was a soldier and a man fascinated by ships. He campaigned both in the Western Isles and on the Anglo-Scottish Borders, capturing and losing castles and towns.

1.   Sauchieburn
2.   Port of Leith
3.   Dunstaffnage Castle
4.   Norham Castle
7.   Etal Castle
8   Ford Castle
9.   Flodden
10.   Twizellhaugh
11.   Coldstream
13.   Burgh Muir, Edinburgh
14.   Ellemford
15.   Tillicoultry
16.   Dunblane
17.   Lochmaben
19.   Isle of May

Map 3: Military

Chapter 12: James IV: Two Book Reviews

The last biography published of James IV was Norman Macdougall's James IV in 1997. The anniversary of Flodden in 1513 brought several books about the battle to the market, and there has also been a study of the whole Tudor and Stewart relationship. All of the writers bring James IV to life in different ways, looking at how his strong character shaped events.

Fatal Rivalry: Flodden 1513

Author: George Goodwin

Publisher: Weidenfeld & Nicolson (4 July 2013)

In a nutshell: An excellent retelling of this seminal battle in the Anglo-Scottish wars which will interest a far wider audience than just those interested in military history.

Books about military campaigns are often hard to follow as armies march hither and thither in terrain that may have changed out of all recognition since the event. Goodwin's writing style, however, is so fluid and fluent that the reader has no trouble at all finding out what happened at this most traumatic of battles. The book is not just a dry account of a battle, but describes in detail the personalities of the men (and women) involved, giving details of their courts, and their parallel approaches to displaying their wealth and power.

One of the best aspects of Goodwin's work is the firm placing of the battle of Flodden in its European context. Usually, the battle is only considered as another round in the endless Anglo-Scottish wars, but, in fact, it can be seen as one of the components of the War of the League of Cambrai.

The account opens with the succession of James VI to the English throne, some ninety years after the battle itself. It then backtracks to the early years of the reign of the Scottish King James IV, and examines the relationships between him, and, first, Henry VII, then Henry VIII of England.

Both James IV and Henry VII won their crowns in battle. Unlike the majority of renaissance princes, Henry was not naturally warlike, although he proved himself competent in war as in everything else. James, on the other hand, was keen to unite his factious nobles in the time-honoured way of annoying his southern neighbours. He therefore began the first of his three Border campaigns through support of the imposter, Perkin Warbeck, who claimed to have a better right to the English throne than Henry VII. Goodwin covers the wider diplomatic ambitions of James to be recognised as a player on the European stage by such illustrious monarchs as the Holy Roman Emperor, Maximilian I, and the Catholic Kings of Spain.

Having dealt with the diplomatic aspects, James followed up with a quick and very successful campaign in Northumberland, that, handily for a monarch who was not overburdened with wealth, paid for itself.

Henry VII, seriously alarmed by James' success, overreacted to a degree that almost cost him his throne. He raised such a huge army to counteract the Scottish threat that the necessary taxation led to rebellion in Cornwall. The peril was so great the Henry was obliged to send his family to the Tower of London and was quite unable to lead an army north.

Always quick to learn, Henry decided on a different strategy to deal with his northern neighbours and sent a senior member of his council,

Bishop Richard Fox of Durham, to negotiate. Keen to prove that he had the upper hand, James promptly besieged Fox in Norham Castle! Backup arrived for Fox in the shape of the Earl of Surrey, but after a little skirmishing, James emerged the victor.

James could now negotiate from a position of strength, and Goodwin describes the various complexities surrounding agreeing a peace between two countries that each had factions opposing a settlement. Also in the mix was a third group in the shape of the Border Reivers who had no interest in the rule of law being imposed by either King.

The long term treaty eventually signed was the Treaty of Perpetual Peace which was to be cemented by the marriage of Henry VII's daughter, Margaret, to James IV in 1503. Again, Goodwin explains all of the ramifications of the treaty in depth, whilst retaining the reader's interest.

Despite some minor incursions into both countries by the other, the Treaty of Perpetual Peace held for the rest of Henry VII's life. Matters changed, however in 1511. By that time, Henry VII had been succeeded by Henry VIII, brother of James' wife. Henry VIII was a whole different kettle of fish from his father. Impetuous where his father had been prudent, warlike where his father had been peace-loving, and, most of all, extravagant where his father had been parsimonious, the young Henry VIII was eager to prove his military mettle.

This leads us into the meat of the book – the early sea skirmishes, the arguments over Henry VII's bequest to his daughter, Margaret, Queen of Scots that was withheld, the blandishments of the French King in his quest to encourage James to remember the older treaty with France rather than the Treaty of Perpetual Peace, and finally, the desire of both Kings to prove themselves in war.

Goodwin describes the preparations for military action, the increasingly belligerent war of words in 1511-1513, and finally, the campaign itself. Despite knowing the outcome of the battle, its depiction is nail-bitingly suspenseful as the moves and countermoves of James and his opponent across Northumberland are retold, the relative strengths of the two armies measured, and the final result explained.

Highly recommended!

*

Flodden: A Scottish Tragedy

Author: Peter Reese

Publisher: Birlinn Ltd (4th July 2013)

In a nutshell: A really thorough examination of the military position of Scotland both before and during the reign of James IV, and a detailed description of the Flodden campaign.

This book sets the campaign of Flodden in its military context, as much as its political one. The first section of the book outlines the progress of the endless border campaigns fought between Scotland and England and the military issues that decided the outcome of each. Essentially, England could command more money, more arms and more men, but Scottish resistance was fierce, and, provided the Scots could wait a long invasion out, they could eventually repel the English. England, although richer, had neither the resources, nor the sustained will to permanently conquer and settle its northern neighbour.

The Scottish Kings played a dangerous game. As well as repelling English invasions, they often had an eye to extending the border south, claiming the ancient kingdom of Northumbria was subject to the Scots Crown. The prize most bitterly fought over was Berwick, which, although originally Scots, changed hands some thirteen times in all. In the 1460s it was ceded to Scotland by Marguerite of Anjou, the Lancastrian Queen, in return for troops, but was grabbed back a final time by Richard, Duke of Gloucester (later Richard III).

Reese then moves on to the events of James IV's reign and his relationship with Henry VII, the final victor in the Wars of the Roses and his flamboyant son, James' brother-in-law, Henry VIII.

James IV's development of artillery and the effective use of cannon in suppressing the early rebellions of his realm are touched on, then the very effective campaign of 1497. This provoked a more aggressive response than James had, perhaps, anticipated and it was lucky for James that Henry was diverted by the Cornish rising.

Following the 1497 campaign, and the eventual Truce of Ayton, war between the countries ceased, in principle at least, although low level border incursions continued. This period of peace was seized on by James to increase Scottish naval capability, and Reese looks at this in some depth.

Reese asks the interesting question of whether James' success in the early part of his reign led him to believe that his military strength was greater than was actually the case. He also points out that some of James' expenditure on his trophy ships might have been better spent on a fund for paying soldiers' wages, or mercenaries, to allow him to raise an army that was both larger, and longer-lasting than reliance on the feudal levies. James was, however, a mediaeval king and thought in terms of military service, rather than a paid army.

We then come to the deterioration of relations between the two countries in the period 1509 – 1513. Reese explores the sometimes similar, sometimes competing, characters of James IV and Henry VIII, and the effect their outlook and personalities had on political and military matters. He also looks at the Battle of Flodden in the context of wider European issues.

In his concentration on military matters, Reese does not always examine some of the political nuances that other writers consider in more detail, but he does look at the importance of military success to both kings, but particularly James, in preserving their positions in a society that fundamentally considered success in battle as the most important element of kingship.

Reese's real contribution is the detailed analysis of the battle preparations, the different methods raising of troops and how they were supplied and paid, the relative merits of the various weapons that the two armies deployed, the skill and experience of the commanders, and finally, the battle itself.

In all, a very thorough and readable account of a battle that had a major effect on the history of the British Isles.

Bibliography

Accounts of the Treasurer of Scotland: v. 5-8:. Edinburgh: H.M. General Register House, 1877

Calendar of State Papers Simancas, British History Online (HMSO, 1892) Hume, Martin A S, ed.,

Calendar of State Papers: Venice <http://www.british-history.ac.uk/cal-state-papers/venice/vol2/vii-lxi> [accessed 7 October 2015]

Charters and Documents Relating to the City of Glasgow 1175 - 1649, *British History Online* <http://www.british-history.ac.uk/glasgow-charters/1175-1649/no2/pp79-87> [accessed 17 September 2015]

Letters and Papers, Foreign and Domestic, of the Reign of Henry VIII: Preserved in the Public Record Office, the British Museum, and Elsewhere in England (United Kingdom: British History Online, 2014) https://www.british-history.ac.uk/letters-papers-hen8/ Brewer, John Sherren, and James Gairdner,

De Lisle, Leanda, *Tudor: The Family Story* (United Kingdom: Chatto & Windus, 2013)

Drummond, William, ed., *The History of Scotland from the Year 1423 until the Year 1542, Containing the Lives and Reigns of James I, II, III, IV and V* (London: H Hills for R Tomlins and himself, 1655)

Ellis, Henry, *Original Letters, Illustrative of English History: Including Numerous Royal Letters: From Autographs in the British Museum, the State Paper Office, and One or Two Other Collections.*, 1st edn (New York: Printed for Harding, Triphook, & Lepard, 1824)

Fraser, Antonia, *Mary Queen of Scots* (London: HarperCollins Publishers, 1970)

Goodwin, George, *Fatal Rivalry, Flodden 1513: Henry VIII, James IV and the Battle for Renaissance Britain,* ebook (London: Weidenfeld & Nicolson)

Hall, Edward, *Hall's Chronicle.* (S.l.: Ams Press, 1909)

Harris, George, *James IV: Scotland's Renaissance King* (Lectures in Scottish History Book 4), Kindle, 2013

Holinshed, Raphael, *Holinshed's Chronicles of England, Scotland & Ireland* (United Kingdom: AMS Press, 1997)

Jerdan, William, ed., *Rutland Papers. Original Documents Illustrative of the Courts and Times of Henry VII and Henry VIII. Selected from the Private Archives of His Grace the Duke of Rutland* (Leopold Classic Library, 2015)

Lang, Andrew, *The History of Scotland from the Roman Occupation: Vol III C. 79 - 1545*, 3rd edn (New York: Dodd, Mead & Co., 1903)

Lindsay of Pitscottie, Robert, *Pitscottie's Chronicles of Scotland*, ed. by Ae. J. G Mackay (Edinburgh: Blackwood for the Society, 1911)

Marshall, R. K. (2003) *Scottish Queens 1034 - 1714*. United Kingdom: Tuckwell Press.

http://www.nas.gov.uk/downloads/jamesIIIDeath.pdf [accessed 17 September 2015]

Oliver, Neil: *A History of Scotland* (Phoenix PR, 2011)

Pitcairn, Robert: *Criminal Trials in Scotland from AD 1488 to AD 1624* (Edinburgh: William Tait, 1833)

Perry, Maria, *Sisters to the King*, 2nd edn (Andre Deutsch, 2002)

Porter, Linda, *Crown of Thistles: The Fatal Inheritance of Mary Queen of Scots* (United Kingdom: Macmillan, 2013)

Records of the Parliaments of Scotland <http://www.rps.ac.uk/> [accessed 17 September 2015]

Reese, Peter, *Flodden: A Scottish Tragedy (Birlinn)* (Edinburgh: Birlinn Publishers, 2003)

Reid, Stuart, *Battles of the Scottish Lowlands* (Barnsley: Pen & Sword Military, 2004)

Strickland, Agnes: *Lives Of The Queens Of Scotland And English Princesses: Connected With The Regal Succession Of Great Britain* (Harper & Brothers, 1859), i & ii

Thomson, John Maitland, ed., *The Register of the Great Seal of Scotland* (Edinburgh: HM General Register House, 1894)

Vergil, Polydore, *Anglica Historia AD 1485-1637* (Royal Historical, 1950)

www.tudortimes.co.uk